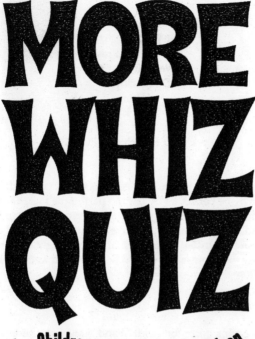

MORE WHIZ QUIZ

For Children and Grown-up Children

Compiled by Cork West Branch
of the NCP-P

The Collins Press

Published in 2007 by
The Collins Press
West Link Park
Doughcloyne
Wilton
Cork

British Library Cataloguing in Publication data.

More whiz quiz : for children and grown-up children
1. Children's questions and answers
I. National Parents' Council (Ireland)
032'.02

ISBN-13: 9781905172504

Typesetting: The Collins Press

Font: Palatino, 11 point

Printed in the UK by Cox and Wyman

ACKNOWLEDGEMENTS

This book has been a wonderfully collaborative effort with assistance from parents, teachers, principals and, most importantly, our wonderful students. It has been a great honour to work on *More Whiz Quiz*. I would like to say thanks to all those parents, students and teachers that assisted in providing questions. I would like to extend a special thanks to the students and staff at Glasheen Boys National School and Glasheen Girls National School in Cork for their questions. I would also like to thank Miss Clark at Glasheen Boys School for her assistance with the Irish questions. We have included questions about every county and at every level so kids of all ages from junior infants to 100 will be able to participate at some level. We at the Cork West National Parents Council are very pleased to be able to provide another *Whiz Quiz* book for all to enjoy and hope it will be fun. I would like to thank Marthe Mainerich, committee member, for co-ordinating this project.

Thank you for your support.
SEAN O'RIORDAN, CHAIRMAN
NATIONAL PARENTS COUNCIL – CORK WEST

Quiz Number 1

Round 1

1. What do you have to do to find a pot of gold?

2. In what year did Christianity come to Ireland?

3. What is Ireland's smallest county?

4. Who won the All-Ireland Hurling Final in 2004?

5. What does www stand for in an Internet address?

6. Who wrote the Harry Potter book series?

7. What tree, that has green leaves and red berries, is associated with Christmas?

8. Who hosts *Winning Streak* on RTÉ television?

Answers on page 101

Round 2

1. What is fossilised wood called?

2. On which continent is the highest active volcano?

3. What is the name of Australia's largest lake?

4. What Irish player captained the Lions in 2005?

5. In what fabled land did Oisín live with his wife Niamh?

6. In the cartoon *Yu-Gi-Oh*, from what ancient civilisation did Duel Monsters originate?

7. What is a tricephalos?

8. In which county is the Blarney Stone?

Answers on page 101

ROUND 3

1. Whose body was wrapped in the Turin Shroud?

2. What is the name of the mouse in Bear's Big Blue House?

3. How many talismans did the Tuatha Dé Danann bring to Ireland on their mystic cloud?

4. What is the only island that lemurs naturally live upon?

5. Who was the first woman to be chairperson of the Irish Red Cross?

6. In what year was the Easter Rising?

7. Which racecourse hosts the Irish Derby?

8. In a solar or lunar eclipse does the Moon pass between the Sun and Earth?

Answers on page 101

Round 4

1. In what year was the Council of Europe founded?

2. What is Spiderman's other identity?

3. What do the letters NPC-P stand for?

4. What is pictured on the back of an Irish one Euro coin?

5. How many times would you press the number 9 to text the letter y?

6. In what film does Eddy Murphy lend his voice to a cartoon dragon?

7. What colours are the German flag?

8. In what year was the Gaelic Athletic Association founded?

Answers on page 101

ROUND 5

1. How many times has Ireland won the Eurovision Song Contest?

2. Canberra is the capital of which country?

3. Who was the first Christian missionary sent to Ireland by the Pope?

4. Who was the first Irish-American Catholic president of the United States of America?

5. What is the European Economic Community now known as?

6. Which Irish band has a song on the soundtrack of *Spiderman 3*?

7. What is a baby elephant called?

8. What is the bottom number in a fraction called?

Answers on page 101

ROUND 6

1. How many counties are in the province of Leinster?

2. What is the name of the Egyptian goddess of healing and marriage?

3. Where would you find your fibula?

4. What is the term describing a piece of music in which a short melody or phrase is introduced by one part and taken up and developed by others?

5. What kind of sea creature is SpongeBob's friend Patrick?

6. Which Dublin born author wrote *Gulliver's Travels*?

7. Which mountain in Kerry is traditionally climbed on the Feast of St Brendan?

8. How long were the children of King Lir turned into white swans?

Answers on page 101

ROUND 7

1. How many miles are in a marathon?

2. What is the name of the Irish hand-held, goatskin drum?

3. When did Wolfe Tone die?

4. Where was George Bernard Shaw born?

5. What are Ron Weasley's twin brothers' names in Harry Potter?

6. Where did the *Lusitania* go down?

7. What kind of animal is Martin the Warrior?

8. In which county is The Giant's Ring?

Answers on page 102

ROUND 8

1. Which team did Damien Duff play for in the 2006-2007 season?

2. Who wrote *Northern Lights* and *The Amber Spyglass*?

3. In what year was the smoking ban introduced in Ireland (2003, 2004 or 2005)?

4. Does an omnivore eat only meat?

5. What character could turn invisible in *The Incredibles*?

6. Asunción is the capital of which country?

7. A doe gives birth to what?

8. What county is also the name of a type of poetry?

Answers on page 102

Round 9

1. In Greek mythology, what is the name of Daedalus' son who fell into the sea?

2. Why did Daedalus' son fall into the sea?

3. Where do you find an incisor?

4. Which character does George McMahon play in *Fair City*?

5. In golf, what does the term 'Eagle' mean?

6. Who is the manager of Sunderland AFC?

7. What does 'I.T.' stand for?

8. The Austrian and French flags share two colours. What are they?

Answers on page 102

Round 10

1. What is the faun's name in *The Lion, the Witch and the Wardrobe*?

2. What horse won the Grand National in 2007?

3. Who wrote *Tom Crean – Ice Man*?

4. What is 14 squared?

5. In which county would you find the Bective Abbey ruins?

6. What is a baby kangaroo called?

7. *Céard a itheann an chaora*?

8. When cooking a roux, what are your two main ingredients?

Answers on page 102

QUIZ NUMBER 2

ROUND 1

1. Which province has 6 counties?

2. What nationality was the first woman elected to the British Parliament?

3. Who was the first woman elected to the British Parliament?

4. In what year did Sonia O'Sullivan with the Silver medal in the Sydney Olympics?

5. How many millilitres are in a teaspoon?

6. In Egyptian history, who was the chief wife of the pharaoh Amenophis IV (Akhenaten)?

7. What are the sections of the spinal column called?

8. What provided the most energy in *Monsters, Inc.*?

Answers on page 103

ROUND 2

1. What results in a higher number: squaring -4 or squaring 3?

2. Was Socrates Greek or Roman?

3. What is the capital of Argentina?

4. In *Scooby-Doo* what colour is Daphne's hair?

5. Did velociraptors live during the Triassic, Jurassic or Cretaceous Period?

6. In Genesis, Lot's wife transformed into what?

7. *Cad é an focal beárla do Ór?*

8. Which animal is found in Ireland: mole, weasel, or wood mouse?

Answers on page 103

ROUND 3

1. Who was the wife of the Greek god Zeus?

2. Coolaney is found in which county?

3. In which show does Tinki Winki appear?

4. How many times has Ireland won the Eurovision Song Contest?

5. Which planet's rings were discovered in 1986 by the *Voyager* 2 space probe?

6. What does the acronym ISPCA stand for?

7. What is the common ratio of oats to liquid when making porridge?

8. In what century did the Vikings invade Ireland?

Answers on page 103

ROUND 4

1. In what year did the Anglo-Normans gain control of Ireland?

2. Where would you go to meet Fungi, the dolphin?

3. St Brigid was born in 454 at an Iron Age hill fort. What was its name?

4. What is painter Rembrandt's family name?

5. What happened to stop the war in the Middle East between the Lydian people and the Medes on 28 May 585 BC?

6. In 1982, which car manufacturers closed in Belfast after just four years of running?

7. Paul Hewson is better known by what name?

8. In which province is the Giant's Causeway?

Answers on page 103

Round 5

1. Lorraine Keane hosts an entertainment show on TV3. What is its name?

2. Complete this verse from 1 Timothy 6:10: 'For the _____ of money is the root of all sorts of evil ...'

3. What is Eragon in the book and film of the same name?

4. What is the capital of Ethiopia?

5. Are iguanas carnivores, omnivores or vegetarians?

6. When did the Iron Age reach Ireland?

7. What is the Irish term used to describe an artificial island built in a lake?

8. Where would you go to see Ossian's Grave?

Answers on page 103

ROUND 6

1. According to the Bible, where did Cain go to live after he killed Abel?

2. What colour is the flower of the thrift?

3. The chough is a rare species of what common bird?

4. In what year did the first coach service begin in Ireland?

5. In which county is Ballymore?

6. Who read the Proclamation of the Republic on the steps of the GPO in Dublin during the 1916 Easter Rising?

7. In which county is The Burren?

8. What is the largest lake on the Shannon?

Answers on page 103

ROUND 7

1. Which layer of a rain forest is highest: understory, emergents or canopy?

2. In what year was Daniel O'Connell born?

3. What time is a quarter past 8pm on the 24-hour clock?

4. What name did Setanta take later in life?

5. Edward Teach was better known by what feared name?

6. Who painted *The Scream*?

7. What colours are on the Czech flag?

8. In what year was Dublin Zoo opened?

Answers on page 104

Round 8

1. In what year did the Wexford rebellion begin?

2. What do you call a young bear?

3. How many holes are there on a golf course?

4. In what year did Christopher Columbus discover America?

5. Who painted the *Water Lilies*?

6. Who wrote *Charlie and the Chocolate Factory*?

7. Who discovered Tutankhamun's Tomb?

8. Does Ogham script, found in fifth- and sixth-century Ireland, have lines and curves or just lines?

Answers on page 104

Round 9

1. In what country did the Tour de France start in 1998?

2. Who was the servant of King Nebuchadnezzar that could understand dreams and visions?

3. What was the name of the first dog in space?

4. What did Pope John Paul II add to the rosary in 2002?

5. During David Beckham's first season at Manchester United, which team was he loaned to?

6. Which city was the European Capital of Culture in 2005?

7. Mount Everest is a part of which mountain range?

8. What Kerryman was a famous Antarctic explorer?

Answers on page 104

ROUND 10

1. Which country had the first street lights?

2. Who wrote the Famous Five books?

3. On which continent is the world's largest rain forest?

4. How many zeros in a googol?

5. When was the launch of TV3?

6. What kind of animal is Dustin on RTÉ's The Den?

7. What Irish organisation sent veterans to assist in the 1865 and 1867 Fenian risings?

8. Who built the lost city of Manchu Picchu?

Answers on page 104

QUIZ NUMBER 3

ROUND 1

1. What footballer player holds the record for the highest ever transfer fee?

2. Antonio Stradivari is famous for making what musical instrument?

3. Are your kidneys located above or below your stomach?

4. Who was the first woman to be president of Ireland?

5. Who established the Plantation Programme in Ireland?

6. In what province was the 1582 Desmond Rebellion?

7. What is the name of Nemo's father in *Finding Nemo*?

8. *San Rann ... Cé d'imigh leis an spúnóg?*

Answers on page 105

Round 2

1. What famous Fianna gained wisdom by sucking his thumb?

2. What was the canvas sunshade for the Roman Colosseum called?

3. What is the name of the passage tomb built in the Boyne Valley during the Neolithic Period?

4. Name the instrument with a long neck and six strings that you strum or pluck with your fingers.

5. In what year did the civil registration of all births, marriages and deaths become compulsory?

6. Anime refers to cartoons from which country?

7. How many members are in the Seanad?

8. Where is harvested barley stored?

Answers on page 105

ROUND 3

1. What is the name of the van that Scooby-Doo and friends ride in?

2. What is the name of the thigh bone?

3. What is the more common name of the Irish fairy also known as *lurgadhan, lurachmaín* or *lurícan*?

4. What is the term used to describe an angle that is greater than 90 degrees?

5. What is impressionist artist Degas' first name?

6. When was the Great Famine?

7. What colour is the €20 note?

8. Which plant, that thrives in wet meadows and marshes, was once used to repel fleas?

Answers on page 105

ROUND 4

1. The Sumerians in Mesopotamia used what number as their basic unit in mathematics?

2. Which Irish county grows the largest amount of apples?

3. What television show featured a portal between Galway and Perth, Australia?

4. Is a whale a fish or a mammal?

5. Which star sign is represented by twins?

6. Which castle was the last Irish stronghold against Cromwellian forces?

7. The Gap of Dunloe was created by what?

8. According to Greek mythology, who was the messenger of the gods?

Answers on page 105

ROUND 5

1. Which bird is the fastest, diving at up to 200 kilometres per hour?

2. Lazarus had two sisters who sent for Jesus when he fell ill, what were their names?

3. What do you call a tradesperson who makes objects out of metal?

4. How do you say buttercup in Irish?

5. Tuesday's child is full of what?

6. What are Sabrina's aunts' names in the television series *Sabrina The Teenage Witch*?

7. What is the capital of France?

8. What do you call a person who studies monkeys?

Answers on page 105

ROUND 6

1. What do the people who live on Easter Island call it?

2. In which county are the Aillwee Caves?

3. What piece of jewellery has a pair of hands, a heart and a crown?

4. Which two ingredients are mixed together to make mortar?

5. Where is the Albert Memorial Clock Tower?

6. What mythical creature has a human head, torso and arms on the body of a horse?

7. Powerscourt lies at the foot of what mountain in County Wicklow?

8. What boy has fairy godparents on the show *Fairly Odd Parents*?

Answers on page 105

Round 7

1. Where is the Tara Brooch now kept?

2. What is the name given to the specially heated building designed to house birds?

3. Where does the Polar Express take children?

4. What symbol of Judaism was once referred to as, 'the seal of Solomon'?

5. During what month is the Pan Celtic Festival celebrated in Tralee?

6. What river runs through Dublin?

7. Was King James II Catholic or Protestant?

8. Mulan is a legendary figure from what country?

Answers on page 106

Round 8

1. What animal can run at speeds of up to 60 kilometres per hour?

2. What is the Irish term used to describe a water-filled pit used for cooking during the Bronze Age?

3. Which country is the largest exporter of beef in the Northern Hemisphere?

4. What is the longest river in Ireland?

5. What tree is considered the symbol of County Derry?

6. In the rhyme 'Sing a song of sixpence' how many blackbirds were baked in a pie?

7. What is the name of Homer Simpson's local pub?

8. Which chess piece can only move diagonally?

Answers on page 106

ROUND 9

1. Which artist painted the *Mona Lisa*?

2. The eagle, the kite and the osprey are all members of what family?

3. What system of writing did ancient Egyptians use?

4. Which sailor and explorer was Mount Brandon named after?

5. Where did Shrek and Fiona stay on their honeymoon?

6. Where is the Hogan Stand?

7. What is Dublin city's telephone area code?

8. What actor stars in *Malcolm in the Middle* and *Agent Cody Banks*?

Answers on page 106

ROUND 10

1. Who hosts News2Day on Den TV?

2. What device allows you to digitally store and play hundreds of songs?

3. If you are facing north and turn right 135 degrees, what direction will you be facing?

4. How many lines are in a Haiku verse?

5. Which city in County Wexford holds a famous Strawberry Fair every year?

6. What does an anemometer measure?

7. What is the capital of India?

8. Robert Emmet was hanged in what year?

Answers on page 106

Quiz Number 4

Round 1

1. What is the name of the process where milk is heated and cooled very quickly to kill harmful germs?

2. In which county is Brí Léith, home of King Mídir?

3. What is the name of the volcano that buried Pompeii when it erupted 79AD?

4. Which character on *Fair City* does Shane McDaid play?

5. What rhyming scheme does a Limerick have?

6. What is the name of the car race that takes place in May around the Lakes of Killarney?

7. What western star sign is represented by a lion?

8. What sport does Setanta O'Halpin now play, since leaving the Cork hurling team?

Answers on page 107

Round 2

1. Who painted the ceilings of St Patrick's Hall in Dublin Castle?

2. Who hosts *The Café*?

3. Does an acoustic or classical guitar use nylon strings?

4. Where is the mandible on the body?

5. Who wrote *Ulysses*?

6. What famous artist illustrated the 1935 deluxe edition of *Ulysses*?

7. On which continent did the Zuni live?

8. What is the study of the origins of words called?

Answers on page 107

Round 3

1. Do white or brown pelicans live in Europe?

2. Who hosts *The Late Late Show*?

3. What county borders Sligo, Galway and Longford?

4. What is the second longest river in Ireland?

5. What do you rub a needle with to turn it into a compass pointer?

6. In Greek mythology, who was the goddess of wisdom?

7. What wooden device was once used to shackle an individual's hands and head in public?

8. What is the answer when you subtract 642 from 865?

Answers on page 107

ROUND 4

1. What was the first symbol for RTÉ Television?

2. What is the name of the biggest flying bird?

3. Does coffee come from trees or vines?

4. In astronomy, what star is also known as the 'dog star'?

5. What sport does Padraig Harrington play?

6. How many strings does a ukulele have?

7. The Gap of Mamore is on which peninsula?

8. What Cistercian monastery is in County Louth?

Answers on page 107

ROUND 5

1. How many years are celebrated on a silver anniversary?

2. What was the capital city of the Aztecs?

3. If doh is a deer, a female deer, what is lah?

4. How many degrees is a right angle?

5. What charitable organisation benefits from the readathon that takes place every year in Ireland?

6. What national route connects Castlebar and Longford?

7. In which county is Birr Castle?

8. W.B. Yeats and Lady Gregory were co-founders of which famous theatre?

Answers on page 107

Round 6

1. What international prize did W.B. Yeats win in 1923?

2. In golf, what does the term 'Birdie' mean?

3. What were commoners called in ancient Rome?

4. How many Teachtaí Dála are in the Dáil?

5. What character on *Fair City* does Jim Bartley play?

6. Which is larger, the violin or the viola?

7. In which country was the Gundestrup Cauldron depicting Cúchulainn found?

8. What was the name of Fionn MacCumhaill's dog?

Answers on page 107

ROUND 7

1. Who wrote *Dracula*?

2. What county is jockey Kieran Fallon from?

3. What is the name of Harry Potter's godfather?

4. What does RNA stand for?

5. How old was Cúchulainn when he killed Culainn the Smith's hound?

6. In what year did Pope John Paul II visit Ireland?

7. What Irish singer organised the Live Aid and Live 8 concerts?

8. Where is the Book of Durrow kept?

Answers on page 108

ROUND 8

1. Who wrote the Goosebumps series of book?

2. When is the main potato crop harvested, mid to late summer or mid to late autumn?

3. Which apostle was martyred first, James or Stephen?

4. In what year was Éire's name changed to the Republic of Ireland?

5. Who was the Irish president when John F. Kennedy visited Ireland?

6. Who won the Tour de France in 1987?

7. What is the largest species of penguin?

8. Are the Galápagos Islands east or west of South America?

Answers on page 108

ROUND 9

1. In the books by Enid Blyton, what tree is regularly visited by different lands, such as the Land of Spells and the Land of Topsy-turvy?

2. *The Wind That Shakes the Barley* covers two significant periods of Irish history. Name one of them.

3. Name the castle in County Meath that is popular as a concert venue.

4. Who is the patron saint of children?

5. Where was President Mary McAleese, née Leneghan, born?

6. What is the capital of Turkey?

7. Mnemosyne is the Greek goddess of what?

8. What is the abbreviation for gold on the Periodic Table of Elements?

Answers on page 108

ROUND 10

1. What does the name hippopotamus mean?

2. What was the most popular pet in ancient Egypt?

3. Who were the original lead dancers in *Riverdance*?

4. In what year did hunger-striker Bobby Sands die?

5. What language is the Book of Kells written in?

6. Birr Castle is in which county?

7. What does the word 'gospel' mean?

8. *Cé chuir eagla ar Ms Muffet*?

Answers on page 108

QUIZ NUMBER 5

ROUND 1

1. How many entrances did the Roman Colosseum have?

2. Name two of *Sattitude*'s hosts.

3. According to legend, Culainn was the blacksmith of which king?

4. St Patrick worked as a slave, herding sheep and pigs, in which county?

5. What metal would you use to kill a werewolf?

6. Which angel was sent by God to tell Zachariah that Elizabeth was to have a son named John?

7. Name the largest bird in the animal kingdom.

8. *Cén fáth ar imigh Jack agus Jill suas an cnoc?*

Answers on page 109

ROUND 2

1. Turlough O'Carolan played what instrument?

2. Emma O'Driscoll is the presenter on what programme?

3. Which leaf is larger, a rowan or elder?

4. What attribute did Roman soldiers hope to gain by wearing a bulb of garlic around their necks?

5. How many stepsisters did Cinderella have?

6. According to legend, who told Fionn not to eat the Salmon of Knowledge?

7. Is Clonmacnois on the bank of the River Shannon or the River Blackwater?

8. In 1947, a statue of who was removed from the front of the Irish Parliament in Dublin?

Answers on page 109

Round 3

1. According to legend, did Grace O'Malley shave her head so she could be a soldier or a sailor?

2. What dog is the mascot for Bus Éireann?

3. In what county is the Glen of the Downs?

4. Who was the first Roman emperor?

5. What is the name of the chalice that Jesus drank from at the Last Supper?

6. Who was Maeve of Connacht's husband?

7. In *Charlotte's Web*, name the famous pig.

8. What do the letters GAA stand for?

Answers on page 109

ROUND 4

1. Complete this saying, 'Early to bed and early to rise ...'

2. Who did Chandler Bing marry on *Friends*?

3. Where would you find the pectoralis muscle?

4. Errigal Mountain is a part of which mountain range in Donegal?

5. Who wrote *The Carnival of Animals* musical score?

6. Peig Sayers is famous for writing about which islands?

7. How long was the lease Arthur Guinness signed in 1759 for the St James' Gate Brewery: 9 years, 900 years or 9,000 years?

8. In which county is the Kells Monastery?

Answers on page 109

Round 5

1. Who plays Suzanne Doyle on *Fair City*?

2. In which county in Ireland is John F. Kennedy's ancestral home?

3. Does car registration KY stand for Kilkenny or Kerry?

4. In which county is Boyle Abbey?

5. In which city is the Parthenon located?

6. Where does the monster Nessie live?

7. Name Batman's butler.

8. What is the start of a river called?

Answers on page 109

ROUND 6

1. Which county is children's television presenter Mary Kingston from?

2. According to legend, how many sons did Parthalón have?

3. Which Ninja Turtle has a purple bandana?

4. Which of the River Shannon's great lakes borders Roscommon, Westmeath and Longford?

5. According to legend, who is the sun god of the Tuatha Dé Danann?

6. Who beat Ireland in the last sixteen of the World Cup 2002?

7. What was the pirate queen Granuaile's given name?

8. What is the capital of Peru?

Answers on page 109

ROUND 7

1. Which king did Joseph and Mary have to flee from with baby Jesus?

2. Who hosts *Wakey Wakey* on The Den?

3. What is papier mâché made from?

4. Ballynahinch, Kilkeel and Dromore are in which county?

5. Which goddess is said to be buried under the cat stone at the Hill of Uisneach, Westmeath?

6. The Four Courts and the Custom House in Dublin were designed by which architect?

7. According to legend, Bandog has what special ability to protect treasure?

8. What kind of animal is Juno on *Pic Me*?

Answers on page 110

ROUND 8

1. What is the name of the sock monster on the Den?

2. Lisbon is the capital of which country?

3. According to legend, Maebh's comb and casket were lost in what Fermanagh lake?

4. What does *Sí Beag* mean?

5. What would you associate terms such as pirouette, arabesque and tutu with ?

6. On *Yu-Gi-Oh*, what is Pegasus' first name?

7. What is more, $^{25}/_{32}$ or $^6/_8$?

8. How many *dúns* (forts) did the hill of Tara have during the time of the high kings?

Answers on page 110

Round 9

1. Name the members of Westlife.

2. In which county is Kylemore Abbey?

3. In which county are the graves of the Children of Lir?

4. Windhoek is the capital of which country?

5. According to legend, who made the Giant's Causeway?

6. According to legend, the Tuatha Dé Danann arrived in Ireland from which country?

7. Is *Tom and Jerry* a MGM, Disney or WB cartoon?

8. Which body of water was Jesus baptised in: Sea of Galilee or the River Jordan?

Answers on page 110

ROUND 10

1. What kind of animal is Snotser?

2. What city is the largest town and ecclesiastical capital of County Donegal?

3. Whose fleets attempted invasions of Bantry in 1689 and 1796?

4. What cars, established in 1815, were Ireland's first transport?

5. Did Moses or Jesus give the 'sermon on the mount'?

6. What number would you press to text the letter 'R'?

7. In which county was famous tenor Count John McCormack born?

8. In what profession is Superman's girlfriend, Lois Lane?

Answers on page 110

QUIZ NUMBER 6

ROUND 1

1. Which two counties does Newry lie in?

2. Lady Betty was a hangman for 30 years in which jail?

3. Who won the All-Ireland Gaelic Football Final in 2006?

4. Who hosts The Club on Den TV?

5. In which county is Ballyshannon?

6. Who writes the Redwall book series?

7. What is the capital of Bolivia?

8. Pigment refers to what trait?

Answers on page 111

ROUND 2

1. What word beginning with d describes the time between day and night?

2. What colour is the Den's puppy Zuppy?

3. Who was the first king of Israel?

4. The thirteenth-century round castle Clogh Oughter is built on an island in which county?

5. Norman Knight, Bertram de Verdon, founded what County Louth town in the twelfth century?

6. In the Harry Potter series of books, who is the Half-Blood Prince?

7. Where was the seat of the high kings of Ulster?

8. In which county was Pierce Butler, an American Constitution signatory, born?

Answers on page 111

ROUND 3

1. When was the Book of Durrow written?

2. What is the capital of Papua New Guinea?

3. Which is the largest inland county in Ireland?

4. What music festival is held annually in Punchestown, County Kildare?

5. *Cé chanann* 'Window in the Skies'?

6. Where is King John's Castle?

7. Where was former president, Mary Robinson, born?

8. Who invented wireless telegraphy?

Answers on page 111

ROUND 4

1. Omagh is located at the foothills of which mountains?

2. In what month is the Monaghan Harvest Time Blues Festival?

3. Which group won Best Irish Band and Best Irish Album at the 2005 Meteor Awards?

4. What mythical beast is half man and half bull?

5. What well-known Irish band manager was a judge on a UK talent show?

6. Where were the first potatoes in Ireland grown by Sir Walter Raleigh?

7. Reginald's Tower and crystal are two things what town is known for?

8. About 10,000 white-fronted geese from Greenland spend winter in this county's wildfowl reserve.

Answers on page 111

ROUND 5

1. In which counties are the Slieve Bloom Mountains?

2. What colours are the Polish flag?

3. Our Lady, St Joseph and St John the Evangelist appeared at what County Mayo town?

4. Where was W.B. Yeats born?

5. In which county is Muckross House found?

6. What is the clavicle better known as?

7. Who is the drummer with U2?

8. St Finbarr is the founder and patron saint of what county capital?

Answers on page 111

ROUND 6

1. Which airport was the world's first duty-free airport?

2. What is the capital of Romania?

3. From which Irish port is the shortest cross-channel passage between Britain and Ireland?

4. Which city was the birthplace of the *Titanic*?

5. What is the capital of County Kerry?

6. What date was the Good Friday Agreement made?

7. What time is a minuet written in?

8. Who is younger, Lisa or Bart Simpson?

Answers on page 111

ROUND 7

1. Clonmel, County Tipperary, is built on which river?

2. Name the castle in County Clare that has been authentically restored and is now a national monument.

3. Who is the patron saint of animals?

4. Which can last longer, a total lunar or total solar eclipse?

5. Which county is Mullingar in?

6. Is Slemish Mountain an extinct volcano?

7. Brian McFadden became famous as a member of which band?

8. Was King Solomon the second, third or fourth king of Israel?

Answers on page 112

ROUND 8

1. Where was the seat of the kings of Leinster?

2. Name the largest Anglo-Irish castle in Ireland?

3. What character does Iain Ó Nuanáin play on *Ros na Rún*?

4. Which river was baby Moses placed in to save his life?

5. In which county was Irish comedian Graham Norton born?

6. What is the capital of Angola?

7. Westport House, which has its own zoo, is located in what county?

8. Hilary Duff stars on what television series?

Answers on page 112

ROUND 9

1. Complete this saying, 'Red sky at night, shepherd's delight. Red sky in the morning ...'

2. On *Tec an Tarracóir*, what is the name of Tec's cow friend?

3. The Ulster Cycle stories are from what age in Ulster: Bronze, Stone, or Iron?

4. The Roman Empire referred to the Irish as *Éire* or *Scoti*?

5. In the Bible, who was Jacob's favourite son?

6. According to legend Fionn learned how to play music from which fairy harper?

7. The holy mountain Croagh Patrick was once known by what name?

8. What is the capital of Libya?

Answers on page 112

Round 10

1. How many colours are in a rainbow?

2. Which county has the largest population?

3. When Tara was home to the high king, how many roads led to it?

4. Name the owner of Clifford the big red dog.

5. *Cén lá Saoire a thiteann ar an tríu Domhnach de mhí Meitheamh?*

6. The top of a mountain is called its what?

7. If you sailed directly west of Ireland what country would you arrive at first?

8. Trim Castle lies beside what river?

Answers on page 112

Quiz Number 7

Round 1

1. How many seats were in the first Dáil?

2. Where in Ireland was the Ryder Cup held in 2006?

3. Dora has to watch out for what fox when she is exploring?

4. What is an otter's home called?

5. Who did King Conor send Cúchulainn to for training on the Isle of Skye?

6. Which river is farther north, the Blackwater or the Suir?

7. The Beaghmore stone circles are found in which county?

8. Managua is the capital of which country?

Answers on page 113

Round 2

1. What did Samson get his strength from?

2. Teachtaí Dála elections are held at least how often?

3. Where would you find a ewe?

4. In the cartoon, what family adopted Poochini the dog?

5. Does the term feline or canine refer to a dog?

6. Which river travels through Lough Neagh?

7. What gift did Scathach give to Cúchulainn?

8. Who is U2's manager?

Answers on page 113

ROUND 3

1. What is the capital of Iceland?

2. In music, what does *a cappella* mean?

3. How many kilometres are there in a mile?

4. The scale used to determine the force of wind was invented by which Navan man?

5. In the cartoon, what brother and sister are able to visit Dragonland?

6. When writing in Ogham would one usually start at the bottom or top of the stone?

7. In which county is Carrigafoyle Castle?

8. Ballinasloe Fair takes place in which month?

Answers on page 113

Round 4

1. What does a meteorologist do?

2. What kind of animal was Splinter on *Teenage Mutant Ninja Turtles*?

3. In what month does salmon fishing season begin?

4. According to the Book of Joshua, which woman in the city of Jericho protected the Israelite spies?

5. What is a squirrel's home called?

6. In which county is Lough Arrow?

7. The town of Bushmills is located in which province?

8. Moraine is made of deposits from glaciers or volcanoes?

Answers on page 113

ROUND 5

1. What is the name of the island formed off the coast of Iceland in 1963?

2. Who plays Rita Finnegan on *Fair City*?

3. Glin Castle is located in which county?

4. What is a rabbit's home called?

5. The letters of the Ogham alphabet are named after what?

6. How long does the mayfly live?

7. What is the name of the Roman goddess of love?

8. In *Yu-Gi-Oh* what is Mai's surname?

Answers on page 113

ROUND 6

1. Name a mountain range in County Waterford.

2. Is the front of a boat called the bow or stern?

3. Copper and tin mixed together make what?

4. Clones is found in what county?

5. What are the stomach muscles called?

6. What is the name of the quiz programme on TG4 where contestants fly from planet to planet?

7. According to legend, who was Nemhedh's wife?

8. What is the capital of Afghanistan?

Answers on page 113

ROUND 7

1. In Tae Kwon Do what coloured belt comes after a white belt?

2. The M50 circles what city?

3. During the Great Plague, in 1664, what herb became more valuable than gold because it was believed to keep the infection away?

4. How long does it take for the earth to move around the sun?

5. On *Hoobs*, who do Iver, Tula and Groove report to?

6. What kind of animal is a wheatear?

7. According to Irish folklore, who warned Irish chieftain Dunlang O'Hartigan, on 23 April 1014, of impending death just prior to the Battle of Clontarf?

8. What leaves were once used to cure boils?

Answers on page 114

Round 8

1. Are the leaves of a water lobelia above or below the water?

2. Name one website that allows you to create your own profile and interact with others.

3. What is the third letter of the Greek alphabet?

4. What river flows through Derry?

5. Oscar Wilde and Samuel Beckett attended what Enniskillen school?

6. What is the name of a pig's home?

7. What is the capital of Chile?

8. When leaving Dublin, what direction is the M4?

Answers on page 114

ROUND 9

1. What kind of home does an Inuit have?

2. In the Stone Age what were clothes made out of?

3. Mount Horeb is more commonly known by what name?

4. What children's television show has characters such as Elmo, the Cookie Monster and Big Bird?

5. The first Viking settlers sailed up the River Bann and settled on the shores of what lough?

6. What type of weapons did the Celts bring to Ireland, iron, bronze or stone?

7. Was King Sitric of Dublin a Viking, Irishman, or Celt?

8. What shape is on the Japanese flag?

Answers on page 114

ROUND 10

1. What instrument is used to study the sun's corona?

2. Fidchell was a Celtic form of what modern board game?

3. When is the Celtic new year, Samhain, celebrated?

4. What is the capital of Venezuela?

5. Who hosted the 2007 Meteor Awards?

6. Which country is the smallest in Europe?

7. *Ní capall an Rí is saighdiúirí an Rí ní feider leo cé hé a chur le chéile aris?*

8. What term is used to describe an angle that is less than 90 degrees?

Answers on page 114

QUIZ NUMBER 8

ROUND 1

1. What is the name of a fox's home?

2. What is the name of the Bronze Age grave markers consisting of three or more standing stones with a large rock as a roof?

3. What instrument does Moe play on *Doodlebops*?

4. What was kept in the Ark of the Covenant to remind the Israelites of God's provision for them while they wandered?

5. What does Megalith mean?

6. What symbol is on the Canadian flag?

7. In which country are the Sphinx and pyramids located?

8. Name the International Arts Festival for Children.

Answers on page 115

ROUND 2

1. What term describes when a seed begins to grow?

2. 'An apple a day' is supposed to keep whom away?

3. Name two of Ireland's airlines.

4. Charleville Castle is in which county?

5. Cape Horn is found at the southern end of which continent?

6. What book won the Dublin Airport Authority Children's Book of the Year at the 2007 Irish Book Awards?

7. What are the ingredients of concrete?

8. *Cén brat atá ar long pirate?*

Answers on page 115

ROUND 3

1. What type of cloud forms rounded masses heaped on each other above a flat base at fairly low altitude?

2. What band is Glen Hansard the lead singer with?

3. What book is between James and Philemon in the New Testament?

4. Athens had the first democracy. Were women permitted to vote?

5. In the time of the ancient Romans, what was the name for Ireland?

6. What is the capital of Guyana?

7. In what county is Carrickfergus Castle?

8. What is 1,703 + 3,041?

Answers on page 115

Round 4

1. What is the piece of wood sewn into the toe of a ballet shoe called?

2. Who plays Jason O'Connor on *Ros na Rún*?

3. The Cape of Good Hope is at the southern end of which continent?

4. Who lit the first fire at the centre of Ireland at Uisneach?

5. The Fir Bolg divided Ireland into how many provinces?

6. What is the highest mountain in Western Europe?

7. What is a group of penguins called?

8. In Roman mythology, who was the leader of all gods?

Answers on page 115

ROUND 5

1. What is the longest river in Europe?

2. The Tuatha Dé Danann were the tribe of which goddess?

3. What is the capital of Lithuania?

4. What mountain range separates Europe and Asia?

5. In myth, the berries eaten by the Salmon of Knowledge came from what kind of tree?

6. Was the famous raider Niall of the 8, 9, or 10 Hostages?

7. Who sings 'July'?

8. How many wings does a bee have?

Answers on page 115

ROUND 6

1. What did the Tuatha Dé Danann Spear of Lugh talisman ensure?

2. What is a herd of more than twelve boars called?

3. What is the longest river in Asia?

4. What teams played in the final of the Champions League in 2007?

5. What is the Irish term for mermaid?

6. Where do Lilo and Stitch live?

7. During the Iron Age, which Irish kingdom included territory in northern Britain and Scotland?

8. What language do deaf people utilise to communicate with their hands?

Answers on page 115

Round 7

1. What mythical artefact would roar or cry out when the right Celtic king was inaugurated?

2. What holiday takes place on the Sunday after the first full moon following the spring equinox?

3. In 867 AD, Ui Néill defeated the Vikings with the Staff of Jesus and what relic?

4. Which is smaller, the African or Asian elephant?

5. Which swims upside down, the Greater Water Boatman or the Pond Skater?

6. What is 75 per cent of 200?

7. What colours are on the Greek flag?

8. In the Harry Potter series of books, are Hermione's parents wizards or muggles?

Answers on page 116

ROUND 8

1. When cooking a basic white sauce what are your three main ingredients?

2. What is the highest mountain in Africa?

3. Why did Bres the Beautiful replace Nuadha as king of the Tuatha Dé Danann?

4. In which county is Blackrock Castle?

5. Is Jack B. Yeats a painter or a poet?

6. Which character becomes Darth Vader?

7. *Cad is naoi meadaithe le naoi?*

8. What is the common term for the oesophagus?

Answers on page 116

ROUND 9

1. Found in 1990 in Dublin, *The Taking of Christ* was painted by what famous artist?

2. What is the longest river in South America?

3. Who wrote the *Star Wars* series?

4. Are plums considered top or soft fruits?

5. How many books are in the New Testament?

6. What battle ended the Nine Years' War?

7. Name one of the three goddesses of Ireland in Celtic times.

8. Is Clew Bay on the north, south, west or east coast of Ireland?

Answers on page 116

ROUND 10

1. The Great Barrier Reef is found off the coast of what continent?

2. What Irish Saint is said to have visited North America about 900 years before Columbus?

3. The emu, kiwi and rhea birds all have what trait in common?

4. What is the first festival of the Celtic year?

5. Is Antarctica at the North or South Pole?

6. What magical animal did St Ciarán of Clonmacnois have?

7. In *Star Wars*, Chancellor Palpatine is known by what Sith name?

8. In music, what Italian term means to play fast and lively?

Answers on page 116

QUIZ NUMBER 9

ROUND 1

1. Who was the first person to reach the South Pole?

2. Which saint founded the Ardmore monastery?

3. What are the names of the two male members of Hi-5?

4. Montevideo is the capital of which country?

5. How many Irish players were on the Lions Touring Party 2005?

6. Which county is named after a plank or board according to legend?

7. What festivals or gatherings held on St Colmcille's Day were outlawed in a 1704 Act of Parliament?

8. The month of August was named after which Roman emperor?

Answers on page 117

ROUND 2

1. What is the name of a doctor who specialises in putting people to sleep before surgery?

2. How many books are in the Old Testament?

3. Which lead character in *Scooby Doo* wears glasses?

4. Who were the first people to settle in New Zealand?

5. Where did Deirdre and her lover flee to escape Conchobhar's wrath?

6. The Pyrenees Mountains lie on the borders of which two countries?

7. Who did the Irish defeat at the Battle of Clontarf in 1014?

8. In which county is Lissadell House?

Answers on page 117

ROUND 3

1. How many witches are usually in a coven?

2. Name one of the two magical schools that competed with Hogwarts in the TriWizard Tournament in the Harry Potter series of books.

3. What does a Giant Panda eat?

4. Which city's name means 'Fort of the Foreigners', after a garrison built by the Vikings?

5. Which character did Liam Neeson play in *Batman Begins*?

6. What is the capital of New Zealand?

7. In which county is Parke's Castle?

8. What word describes a general lack of food?

Answers on page 117

ROUND 4

1. What is the common term for influenza?

2. What astrological sign is represented by the crab?

3. What superheroine did Mr Incredible marry?

4. If the books of the Bible were listed alphabetically, which would come first?

5. What body of water separates Ireland from Scotland?

6. Is a sea campion a fish, flower or bird?

7. What land is Bigfoot or Yeti native to?

8. What does abracadabra mean?

Answers on page 117

Round 5

1. Who did Anakin Skywalker secretly marry contrary to Jedi law?

2. *Chur an abairt seo i gcríoch ... 'Níl aon tinteán ...'*

3. What is a fear of spiders called?

4. In mythology, the Greeks called the god of the underworld Hades. What did the Romans call him?

5. When did the Black Death come to Ireland?

6. In what county is the National Stud?

7. At the end of which month does the Fleadh Cheoil take place?

8. The filbert nut is more commonly known by what name?

Answers on page 117

ROUND 6

1. In what year did Ireland join the United Nations?

2. Is a fez a bird, a pair of trousers or a hat?

3. How many wings does a housefly have?

4. Which political party has been around longer, Sinn Féin, Fianna Fáil or Fine Gael?

5. How often can a queen termite lay an egg?

6. In Greek mythology, what island is the mythical home of the Minotaur?

7. What is Clark Kent's alter ego?

8. How many sides are on a trapezoid?

Answers on page 117

ROUND 7

1. What composer wrote 'Dance of the Sugarplum Fairy'?

2. When was the first successful census in Ireland?

3. Due to a fire at the Public Records office, which is the earliest surviving census of Ireland?

4. What coloured belt follows the high green belt in Tae Kwan Do?

5. Is Jerry the cat or the mouse?

6. Does a stalagmite or stalactite hang from the ceiling of a cave?

7. What is the smallest county in Ireland?

8. Which period did the stegosaurus live in: Triassic, Jurassic or Cretaceous?

Answers on page 118

ROUND 8

1. On which island is the Janus Figure?

2. Where is the oldest maternity hospital in the world?

3. Who painted the ceiling of the Sistine Chapel?

4. What are the names of the twins on Rugrats?

5. Is a treble clef associated with higher or lower notes?

6. What wire kitchen utensil is used to whip eggs or cream by hand?

7. Is Guinness made from rice, barley, or oats?

8. In what county is Fionn MacCumhaill's hurling stone, the Mottee Stone?

Answers on page 118

ROUND 9

1. What is the English name of the county named after the Church of Saint Mantan?

2. In cooking, what is the term used to describe immersing food into boiling water for a short period of time?

3. What is the name of Tracy McBean's brother on her cartoon?

4. What large container would you purchase to house your pet fish?

5. How many arms does an octopus have?

6. Name five of the counties of Leinster.

7. If the books of the Bible were listed alphabetically, which book would be last?

8. Which is larger, the flute or the tin whistle?

Answers on page 118

ROUND 10

1. Do veins bring blood away from or towards the heart?

2. The *Pietà* shows Mary holding the dead body of Jesus. What does the Italian term *pietà* mean?

3. 'Ring a ring a rosie' was sung about those who had what ailment?

4. Black '47 refers to what in Irish History?

5. What did ancient Egyptians use for paper?

6. In what country is the oldest evidence of the Celts found?

7. Which High King of Ireland built a palace at Tara in County Meath?

8. Saint Brigid was known by what name and title in pre-Christian Ireland?

Answers on page 118

Quiz Number 10

Round 1

1. In *Jakers, the Adventures of Piggley Winks*, what are the names of Piggley's grandsons?

2. What insect carries malaria?

3. What would you use to make a St Brigid's Cross?

4. Conchobhar died with whose calcified brain ball sewn in his head?

5. If you had a pet lizard or turtle, what would you call the glass case where he would live?

6. In Biblical times, the prophet Joel saw what creatures devastate Judah as a judgement from God?

7. What is the name describing snakes, turtles, lizards and alligators?

8. Where would you find a mast, lines and boom?

Answers on page 119

ROUND 2

1. A person who can make puppets talk without their lips moving is called what?

2. Who was the mother of Lir's children?

3. What are the names of the girls from Hi-5?

4. Turgesius, Viking invader of the ninth century, was finally killed by which Irish King?

5. What text letters are associated with the number 2 on a mobile?

6. What is the capital of Togo?

7. What is the name of the costume designer for super heroes in *The Incredibles*?

8. Is food digested by the large or small intestine first?

Answers on page 119

Round 3

1. Which county grows the greatest amount of soft fruits in Ireland?

2. What is the name of Pooh's bouncy, striped friend?

3. What is Wicklow's car registration abbreviation?

4. In the Táin Bó Cúailnge, what colour was Cooley's bull?

5. How many branches does a menorah have?

6. Where would you find a ringmaster, tightrope and acrobats?

7. *Cá bhfuil Tadhaigín an tEitleán i gcónaí?*

8. Baffin Bay separates Greenland and what other country?

Answers on page 119

Round 4

1. Are the Ninja Turtles named after musicians, artists or world leaders?

2. Which county is bordered by Counties Kilkenny, Kildare and Offaly?

3. What is the base of a house called?

4. Is a computer program considered hardware or software?

5. A grey crow is also known by what name?

6. What does a barometer measure?

7. Who is the first Ombudsman for Children in Ireland?

8. Was Aristotle Greek or Roman?

Answers on page 119

ROUND 5

1. According to Irish legend, Ciarraí is named after whose son?

2. Who invented the system of printing for the blind?

3. What instrument with two adjustable legs is used to measure thickness of objects or distance between surfaces?

4. In the Redwall series what was Sunstripe's name during his warrior days?

5. Name the planets in our solar system.

6. In *Jakers*, what kind of animal is Dannon?

7. What breakfast food is named after a Roman goddess?

8. How many pieces does each player have at the start of a chess game?

Answers on page 119

Round 6

1. What is the highest mountain in Ireland?

2. In what year did *Titanic* sink?

3. Where did Superman grow up?

4. What Jewish festival celebrates how the Jews were saved from their enemies by Queen Esther?

5. What is the shortest day of the year?

6. Who is the manager of Westlife?

7. When did the first farmers arrive in Ireland?

8. Which character did Hermione attend a formal dance with in *Harry Potter and the Goblet of Fire*?

Answers on page 119

Round 7

1. What is a baby swan called?

2. What is the name of Mr Burns' assistant on *The Simpsons*?

3. Are gannets found inland or on the coasts of Ireland?

4. Is the longest day of the year in June or July?

5. What county lies farther east, Down or Meath?

6. What is an acrophobe afraid of?

7. How many compartments does the heart have?

8. *San Rann ... cé mhéad mala ulann a bhí ag an caora dubh?*

Answers on page 120

Round 8

1. Who directed the *Lord of the Rings* films?

2. What is the heaviest insect in the world?

3. In the Táin Bó Cúailnge, what colour was Ailill's bull?

4. What was the former name of the city of Jerusalem?

5. On *Balamory*, what is the colour of Edie McCredie's Transport?

6. In ancient Rome what kinds of races were held at the Circus Maximus?

7. In which lake did St Patrick kill a monster?

8. Why does Lewis invent a time machine in *Meet the Robinsons*?

Answers on page 120

ROUND 9

1. What is Beyonce's family name?

2. What Irish jockey won the English Grand National in 2007?

3. Who is the Greek god of war?

4. What is the scientific term for the King Tyrant Lizard?

5. Name the muskehounds who fight alongside Dogtanian.

6. What is the capital of Slovakia?

7. What are the names of the Powerpuff Girls?

8. After giving birth to twins, Macha cursed the men of Ulster for how many generations?

Answers on page 120

ROUND 10

1. Who was the only man to ride the pooka (also known as phouka or puca)?

2. When does Rapid Eye Movement (REM) occur?

3. Is the Sea of Galilee a sea, river, lake or ocean?

4. In which county is the Ballykeel Dolmen?

5. What are the names of the Morbegs?

6. Who led the Kilmichael ambush during the war of independence?

7. What was unique about the final of the European Champions League in 2005?

8. According to the Bible, whom did Delilah betray?

Answers on page 120

QUIZ ANSWERS

QUIZ NUMBER 1
ROUND 1
1. Catch a leprechaun
2. 430 AD
3. Louth
4. Cork
5. World Wide Web
6. J.K. Rowling
7. Holly
8. Derek Mooney

ROUND 2
1. Petrified wood
2. South America (it is named Ojos de Salado)
3. Lake Eyre
4. Brian O'Driscoll
5. Tír na nÓg
6. Egyptian
7. A head with three faces
8. Cork

ROUND 3
1. Jesus
2. Tutter
3. 4
4. Madagascar
5. Leslie Bean de Barra
6. 1916
7. The Curragh
8. Solar eclipse

ROUND 4
1. 1949
2. Peter Parker
3. National Parents Council-Primary
4. Harp
5. 3
6. *Mulan*
7. Black, red, and yellow
8. 1884

ROUND 5
1. 7
2. Australia
3. Palladius
4. John F. Kennedy
5. European Union
6. Snow Patrol
7. Calf
8. Denominator

ROUND 6
1. Twelve
2. Isis
3. Leg (it is the ankle bone)
4. Fugue
5. Starfish
6. Jonathan Swift
7. Mount Brandon
8. 900 years

ROUND 7
1. 26
2. *Bodhrán*
3. 18 November 1998
4. Dublin
5. Fred and George
6. Off the Head of Kinsale
7. Mouse
8. Down

ROUND 8
1. Chelsea
2. Philip Pullman
3. 2004
4. No
5. Violet
6. Paraguay
7. Fawn
8. Limerick

ROUND 9
1. Icarus
2. The wax holding the feathers together on his wings melted
3. Mouth (it is a tooth)
4. Mondo
5. A score of 2 strokes under par
6. Roy Keane
7. Information Technology
8. Red and white

ROUND 10
1. Mr Tumnus
2. Silver Birch
3. Michael Smith
4. 196
5. Meath
6. Joey
7. *Féir*
8. Fat and flour

Quiz Number 2

Round 1
1. Munster
2. Irish
3. Countess Constance Markievicz
4. 2000
5. 6 millilitres
6. Nefertiti
7. Vertebrae
8. Laughter

Round 2
1. Squaring -4 (+16)
2. Greek
3. Buenos Aires
4. Orange
5. Cretaceous Period
6. A pillar of salt
7. Gold
8. Wood mouse

Round 3
1. Hera
2. Sligo
3. Teletubbies
4. 7
5. Uranus
6. Irish Society for the Prevention of Cruelty to Animals
7. 1: 2
8. Ninth century

Round 4
1. 1169
2. Dingle, County Kerry
3. Faughart Hill, County Louth
4. Van Rijn
5. A solar eclipse
6. De Lorean
7. Bono – from U2
8. Ulster

Round 5
1. Xposé
2. Love
3. A dragonrider
4. Addis Ababa
5. Vegetarians
6. Third century BC
7. *Crannóg*
8. Tievebulliagh Mountain, County Antrim

Round 6
1. Into exile
2. Pink
3. Crow
4. 1815
5. County Westmeath
6. Patrick Pearse
7. County Clare
8. Lough Derg

ROUND 7
1. Emergents
2. 1775
3. 20.15
4. Cúchulainn
5. Blackbeard
6. Edvard Munch
7. White, blue and red
8. 1830

ROUND 8
1. 1798
2. Cub
3. 18
4. 1492
5. Claude Monet
6. Roald Dahl
7. Howard Carter
8. Lines only

ROUND 9
1. Ireland
2. Daniel
3. Laika
4. Five new Mysteries of
   Light
5. Preston North End
6. Cork
7. Himalayas
8. Tom Crean

ROUND 10
1. Norway
2. Enid Blyton
3. South America
4. 100
5. 20 September 1998
6. Turkey
7. Clan na Gael
8. The Incas

104

Quiz Number 3

Round 1
1. Zinedine Zidane (£45.6 million)
2. Violin
3. Below
4. Mary Robinson
5. King James I
6. Munster
7. Marlin
8. *An baisín*

Round 2
1. Fionn MacCumhaill
2. Velarium
3. Newgrange, 2,500 BC
4. Guitar
5. 1864
6. Japan
7. 60
8. Grain silo

Round 3
1. The Mystery Machine
2. Femur
3. Leprechaun
4. Obtuse
5. Edgar
6. 1845-8
7. Blue
8. Fleabane

Round 4
1. 60
2. County Dublin
3. Foreign Exchange
4. Mammal
5. Gemini
6. Ross Castle, County Kerry
7. Glaciers
8. Hermes

Round 5
1. Peregrine falcon
2. Martha and Mary
3. Blacksmith
4. *Cam an ime*
5. Grace
6. Hilda and Zelda
7. Paris
8. Primatologist

Round 6
1. Rapa Nui
2. County Clare
3. A Claddagh ring
4. Sand and cement
5. Queen's Square, Belfast
6. Centaur
7. Great Sugar Loaf Mountain
8. Timmy

ROUND 7
1. The National Museum, Dublin
2. Aviary
3. The North Pole
4. Star of David
5. April
6. Liffey
7. Catholic
8. China

ROUND 8
1. The cheetah
2. *Fulachta Fiadh*
3. Ireland
4. River Shannon
5. Oak
6. 24
7. Moe's
8. Bishop

ROUND 9
1. Leonardo da Vinci
2. The hawk family
3. Hieroglyphs
4. Saint Brendan
5. Gingerbread Cottage
6. Croke Park
7. 01
8. Frankie Muniz

ROUND 10
1. Helen and Paddy
2. MP3 player/iPod
3. South east
4. 3
5. Enniscorthy
6. The speed of wind
7. New Delhi
8. 1803

Quiz Number 4

Round 1
1. Pasteurisation
2. Longford
3. Mount Vesuvius
4. Stephen
5. aabba
6. International Rally of the Lakes
7. Leo
8. Aussie Rules

Round 2
1. Vincenzo Valdré
2. Aiden and Laura
3. Classical
4. Jaw
5. James Joyce
6. Henri Matisse
7. North America
8. Etymology

Round 3
1. White pelicans
2. Pat Kenny
3. Roscommon
4. Blackwater
5. A magnet
6. Athena
7. Pillory
8. 223

Round 4
1. St Brigid's Cross
2. Albatross
3. Trees
4. Sirius
5. Golf
6. 4
7. Inishowen
8. Mellifont Abbey

Round 5
1. 25
2. Tenochtitlan
3. A note to follow soh
4. 90
5. The Multiple Sclerosis Society of Ireland
6. N5
7. Offaly
8. Abbey Theatre

Round 6
1. Nobel Prize for Literature
2. One stroke under par
3. Plebians
4. 166
5. Bela Doyle
6. Viola
7. Denmark
8. Bran

1. Bram Stoker
2. County Clare
3. Sirius Black
4. Ribonucleic acid
5. 7
6. 1979
7. Bob Geldolf
8. Trinity College, Dublin

ROUND 8
1. R. L. Stine
2. Mid to late autumn
3. Stephen
4. 1949
5. Eamon de Valera
6. Stephen Roche
7. Emperor penguins
8. West

ROUND 9
1. The Magic Faraway Tree
2. The War of Independence and the Civil War
3. Slane
4. St Nicholas
5. Belfast
6. Ankara
7. Memory
8. Au

ROUND 10
1. River horse
2. The cat
3. Michael Flatley and Jean Butler
4. 1981
5. Latin
6. Offaly
7. Good news
8. *An damhán alla*

Quiz Number 5

Round 1
1. 80
2. Molly, Liam, Sinéad and Brian
3. King Conor
4. Antrim
5. Silver
6. Gabriel
7. Ostrich
8. *Chun uisce a fháil*

Round 2
1. Harp
2. Den Tots
3. Elder leaf
4. Strength
5. 2
6. Finegas
7. Shannon
8. Queen Victoria

Round 3
1. Sailor
2. Irish red setter
3. Wicklow
4. Caesar Augustus
5. The Holy Grail
6. Ailill
7. Wilbur
8. Gaelic Athletic Association

Round 4
1. 'makes a man healthy, wealthy and wise'
2. Monica Geller
3. Chest
4. Derryveagh Mountains
5. Caille Saint-Saëns
6. Blasket
7. 9,000
8. Meath

Round 5
1. Sarah McDowell
2. Wexford
3. Kerry
4. Roscommon
5. Athens, Greece
6. Loch Ness, Scotland
7. Alfred
8. Its source

Round 6
1. Cork
2. 4
3. Donatello
4. Ree
5. Lugh
6. Spain
7. Grace O'Malley
8. Lima

ROUND 7
1. Herod
2. Simon Deasy
3. A malleable mixture of paper and glue that becomes hard when dry
4. Down
5. Goddess Ériu
6. James Gandon
7. He has flaming breath
8. Lion

ROUND 8
1. Soky
2. Portugal
3. Lough Erne
4. The Little Fairy Mound
5. Ballet
6. Maximillion
7. $^{25}/_{32}$
8. 7 Dúns (forts)

ROUND 9
1. Kian Egan, Mark Feehily, Shane Filan and Nicky Byrne
2. County Galway
3. Inishglora, County Mayo
4. Namibia
5. Fionn MacCumhaill
6. Greece
7. MGM
8. River Jordan

ROUND 10
1. Pig
2. Letterkenny
3. France's
4. Bianconi cars
5. Jesus
6. 7
7. County Westmeath
8. Journalism

QUIZ NUMBER 6
ROUND 1
1. County Down and County Armagh
2. Roscommon
3. Kerry
4. Kathryn McKiernan.
5. Donegal
6. Brian Jacques
7. La Paz
8. Colour

ROUND 2
1. Dusk
2. Blue
3. Saul
4. Cavan
5. Dundalk
6. Severus Snape
7. Armagh
8. County Carlow

ROUND 3
1. Seventh century
2. Port Moresby
3. Tipperary
4. Oxegen
5. U2
6. Limerick
7. Ballina, County Mayo
8. Guglielmo Marconi

ROUND 4
1. Sperrins
2. September
3. Snow Patrol
4. Minotaur
5. Louis Walsh
6. Youghal, County Cork
7. Waterford
8. Wexford

ROUND 5
1. Laois and Tipperary
2. Red and white
3. Knock
4. Sligo
5. Kerry
6. Collarbone
7. Larry Mullen Junior
8. Cork

ROUND 6
1. Shannon
2. Bucharest
3. Larne, County Antrim
4. Belfast
5. Tralee
6. 10 April 1998
7. Triple time
8. Lisa Simpson

ROUND 7
1. Suir
2. Bunratty Castle
3. St Francis of Assisi
4. Total lunar
5. Westmeath
6. Yes
7. Westlife
8. Third

ROUND 8
1. *Nas na Rí* (Naas), County Kildare
2. Trim Castle
3. Evan Ó Neachtain
4. River Nile
5. Cork
6. Luanda
7. Mayo
8. *Lizzie McGuire*

ROUND 9
1. 'shepherd's warning'
2. Carolyn the Cow
3. Iron Age
4. Scoti
5. Joseph
6. Críu
7. *Cruachan Aigli*
8. Tripoli

ROUND 10
1. 7
2. Down
3. 5
4. Emily Elizabeth Howard
5. *Lá an Athair*
6. Summit
7. Canada
8. River Boyne

Quiz Number 7

Round 1
1. 70
2. The K club
3. Swiper the Fox
4. Holt
5. Scathach
6. Suir
7. Tyrone
8. Nicaragua

Round 2
1. His hair
2. At least once every 5 years
3. On a farm (it is a female sheep)
4. The Whites
5. Canine
6. Bann
7. The *gae bolga* spear
8. Paul McGuinness

Round 3
1. Reykjavik
2. Singing without instrumental accompaniment
3. 1.6
4. Sir Francis Beaufort, 1805
5. Emmy and Max
6. Bottom
7. County Kerry
8. October

Round 4
1. Studies and forecasts the weather
2. Rat
3. January
4. Rahab
5. Drey
6. County Sligo
7. Ulster
8. Glaciers

Round 5
1. Surtsey Island
2. Jean Costello
3. Limerick
4. Burrow
5. Trees, bushes and plants
6. 1 day
7. Venus
8. Valentine

Round 6
1. Comeraghs and Knockmealdowns
2. Bow
3. Bronze
4. Monaghan
5. Abdominals
6. *Cruinneas*
7. Macha
8. Kabul

ROUND 7
1. Yellow
2. Dublin
3. Garlic
4. 365 days
5. Hubba Hubba Hoob
6. Bird
7. The banshee Aoibheall
8. Bogbean

ROUND 8
1. Below the water
2. MySpace, BEBO
3. Gamma
4. Foyle
5. Portora Royal School
6. Sty
7. Santiago
8. West

ROUND 9
1. Igloo
2. Animal skins
3. Mount Sinai
4. Sesame Street
5. Neagh
6. Iron
7. Viking
8. Circle (red)

ROUND 10
1. Coronagraph
2. Chess
3. 1 November
4. Caracas
5. Deirdre O'Kane, Podge and Rodge
6. Vatican City
7. Humpty Dumpty
8. Acute angle

Quiz Number 8

Round 1
1. Den
2. Dolmen
3. Drums
4. A jar of Manna
5. Large stone
6. Maple leaf
7. Giza, Egypt
8. Baboró

Round 2
1. Germination
2. The doctor
3. Aer Arann, Aer Lingus, Ryanair
4. Offaly
5. South America
6. *The Boy in the Striped Pyjamas* by John Boyne, *The Incredible Book Eating Boy* by Oliver Jeffers
7. Sand, gravel, cement and water
8. Jolly Roger

Round 3
1. Cumulus
2. The Frames
3. Hebrews
4. No
5. Hibernia
6. Georgetown
7. Antrim
8. 4,744

Round 4
1. Block
2. Ciabhán Ó Murchú
3. Africa
4. Nemhedh
5. 5
6. Mont Blanc
7. Colony
8. Jupiter

Round 5
1. Volga
2. Goddess Danu (Anu)
3. Vilnius
4. Urals
5. Hazel
6. 9 Hostages
7. Mundy
8. 4

Round 6
1. Victory
2. Sounder
3. Yangtze
4. Liverpool and A.C. Milan
5. *Moruadh* or merrow
6. Hawaii
7. Dalriada
8. Sign language

ROUND 7
1. The Stone of Destiny or Lia Fál
2. Easter
3. A relic of the cross
4. Asian elephant
5. Greater Water Boatman
6. 150
7. Blue and white
8. Muggles

ROUND 8
1. Butter, flour and milk
2. Kilimanjaro
3. Nuadha lost his arm
4. Cork
5. Painter
6. Anakin Skywalker
7. Ochtó a haon
8. Throat

ROUND 9
1. Caravaggio
2. Amazon
3. George Lucas
4. Top fruits
5. 27
6. Battle of Kinsale
7. Banba, Fodhla and Eriu
8. West

ROUND 10
1. Australia
2. Saint Brendan
3. Flightless birds
4. Imbolc
5. South Pole
6. Cow
7. Darth Sidious
8. Allegro

Quiz Number 9

Round 1
1. Roald Amundsen
2. Saint Declan
3. Tim and Nathan
4. Uruguay
5. 11
6. Clare (*An Clár*)
7. Patterns
8. Augustus, Roman emperor

Round 2
1. Anaesthetist
2. 39
3. Velma
4. The Maoris
5. Scotland
6. France and Spain
7. The Vikings
8. Sligo

Round 3
1. 12 witches
2. Beauxbatons and Durmstrang
3. Bamboo
4. Donegal
5. Henri Ducard
6. Wellington
7. Leitrim
8. Famine

Round 4
1. Flu
2. Cancer
3. Elastigirl
4. Book of Acts
5. North Channel
6. Flower
7. Tibet
8. I speak as I create

Round 5
1. Padmé Amidala
2. *'mar do thinteán féin'*
3. Arachnophobia
4. Pluto
5. 1348
6. Tully, County Kildare
7. August
8. Hazelnut

Round 6
1. 1955
2. Hat
3. 2
4. Sinn Féin
5. 1 egg per second
6. Crete
7. Superman
8. 4

ROUND 7
1. Pytor Ilyich Tchaikovsky
2. 1821
3. The 1901 census
4. Low blue belt
5. Mouse
6. Stalactite
7. Louth
8. Jurassic Period

ROUND 8
1. Boa Island
2. Dublin, Rotunda Hospital
3. Michelangelo
4. Phil and Lil
5. Higher notes
6. Whisk
7. Barley
8. Wicklow (atop Cronebane Hill)

ROUND 9
1. Wicklow
2. Blanch
3. Gordon
4. Aquarium
5. 8
6. Carlow, Dublin, Kildare, Kilkenny, Laois, Longford, Louth, Meath, Offaly, Westmeath, and Wicklow
7. Book of Zephaniah
8. Flute

ROUND 10
1. Towards the heart
2. Pity
3. Black Death
4. 1847, the worst year of the Famine
5. Papyrus
6. Hallstatt, Austria, 700 BC
7. Cormac Mac Airt
8. Goddess Bríg

Quiz Number 10

Round 1
1. Seamus and Sean
2. Mosquito
3. Rushes
4. King of Leinster
5. Terrarium
6. Locusts
7. Reptiles
8. On a boat/ship

Round 2
1. Ventriloquist
2. Eva
3. Charli, Kellie and Kathleen
4. King Malachy
5. A, B, C
6. Lomé
7. Edna Mode
8. Small

Round 3
1. Wexford
2. Tigger
3. WW
4. Brown
5. 7
6. At the circus
7. Aerfort Bhaile Teamhrach
8. Canada

Round 4
1. Artists
2. Laois
3. Its foundation
4. Software
5. Scald crow
6. Air pressure
7. Emily Logan
8. Greek

Round 5
1. Fergus and Queen Maeve of Connacht
2. Louis Braille
3. Calipers
4. Sunflash
5. Mercury, Venus, Earth, Mars, Jupiter, Saturn, Uranus, Neptune, Pluto
6. Duck
7. Cereal (Ceres, Goddess of Agriculture)
8. 16

Round 6
1. Carrauntoohil
2. 1912
3. Smallville
4. Purim
5. 21 December, Midwinter Day
6. Louis Walsh
7. 3,700 BC
8. Viktor Krum

ROUND 7
1. Cygnet
2. Smithers
3. Coasts
4. June
5. Down
6. Heights
7. Four
8. *Trí mhala*

ROUND 8
1. Peter Jackson
2. Goliath beetle
3. White
4. Jebus
5. Yellow
6. Chariot races
7. Lough Derg,
8. Because he wants to know what his mother looked like

ROUND 9
1. Knowles
2. Robbie Power
3. Ares
4. Tyrannosaurus Rex
5. Porthos, Athos, Aramis
6. Bratislava
7. Bubbles, Blossom and Buttercup
8. 9

ROUND 10
1. High King of Ireland Brian Boru
2. When one is sleeping
3. Lake
4. Armagh
5. Molly and Rossa
6. Tom Barry
7. It lasted 2 days (25 and 26 May)
8. Samson